My Little Book of Iman

Iman for Little Ones

Shiban Akbar

Ta-Ha Publishers Ltd.

First Edition October 1998
Second Revised Edition January 2005

Published by:
Ta-Ha Publishers Ltd.
1 Wynne Road
London SW9 0BB

Website: http://www.taha.co.uk
Email: sales@taha.co.uk

Written by: Shiban Akbar
General Editor: Dr. Abia Afsar-Siddiqui
Design and Layout: Mariama Janneh

A catalogue record of this book is available from the British
Library.

ISBN 1 842000 62 4

Printed and Bound in England by: De-Luxe Printers Ltd.
Park Royal, London NW10 7NR

We begin in the name of Allah

'**Allah** is the light
Of the heavens and the earth...'
'Light upon light...'

'(The light is found) in houses
By **Allah's** permission
To honour and celebrate His name.'

'In them He is praised morning
And evening.'

(THE QUR'AN 24:35 & 36)

As salaam alaikum, Peace be upon you,
Dear friends!

If you sit tight, I shall tell you some
very nice things.
I shall first tell you about **Allah**.

Who is **Allah**?
Allah is the Lord, the Mighty King
Of the Heavens and the Earth.

To **Allah** belongs
All that is in the Heavens and the Earth.
We all belong to **Allah**.

There is none like **Allah**.
He is the Most High.

When we say **Allah**,
We say *subhanahu wa ta'ala*.
This means *Glory to the Most High*.

Allah is All-Beautiful.
Allah is All-Powerful over everything.
Allah is the Greatest.

Allah gives life,
He makes things happen.

Allah is the Most Kind,
He is the Most Wise.

Allah is the Ever-Living,
He is the Everlasting.

Allah is Forever Awake,
He is Forever Bright.

Allah is Light upon Light.

Now I shall tell you about Islam.
Islam is our religion.
Do you know what Islam means?

The word Islam means
To do as we are told and
To listen to **Allah**.

When we do as **Allah** tells us to do,
We obey Him.

What is **religion?**
Religion is a way of life,
A path that people follow.

Islam is our religion,
Our way of life,
Our path,
To all things good and beautiful.

Those who follow the way of Islam
are called **Muslims**.

Muslims should follow Islam.
To follow means to understand
and to do what we are asked.

What do Muslims believe in?
Muslims believe in Islam as their
Way of Life.
As a Muslim each of us must remember this:

I believe in **Allah**,

آمَنْتُ بِاللهِ

In His **Angels**,

وَمَلَائِكَتِهِ

In His **Books**,

وَكُتُبِهِ

In His **Messengers**,

وَرُسُلِهِ

In the **Last Day**,

وَالْيَوْمِ الْأَخِرِ

In the fact that **Fate**,
both good and bad,

وَالْقَدَرِ خَيْرِهِ وَشَرِهِ

Is from **Allah**,

مِنَ اللهِ تَعَالَى

And in **Life after death**.

وَالْبَعْثِ بَعْدَ الْمَوْتِ

This is **Iman ul Mufassal**
(Faith in Detail)

We know that
Allah is All-Beautiful and All-Powerful.

Every living thing comes from **Allah**.
This is a sign of the power of **Allah**.
It is also a sign of the beauty of **Allah**.
The signs display His beauty and power.

Allah has ninety-nine names.
They are the beautiful names of **Allah**.
They are the excellent names of **Allah**.
Together they are called
Asma-al-Husna.

Each name is a power of **Allah**.
He has many different powers,
So He has many different names.

9

**For now I shall tell you only
Ten of Allah's beautiful names.**

1. Al-Wahid, The One   اَلْوَاحِدُ

2. Al-Awwal, The First   اَلْأَوَّلُ

3. Al-Akhir, The Last   اَلْأَخِرُ

4. Al-Wadud, The Loving   اَلْوَدُودُ

5. Ar-Rauf, The Gentle   اَلرَّؤُوفُ

6. Al-Alim, The All-Knowing   اَلْعَلِيمُ

7. Al-Basir, The All-Seeing   اَلْبَصِيرُ

8. As-Sami, The All-Hearing   اَلسَّمِيعُ

9. As-Salam, The Source of Peace   اَلسَّلَامُ

10. Al-Qadir, The Powerful   اَلْقَادِرُ

Can you remember these names of Allah?

Did you know that
Allah is The Best Designer,
The Best Shaper and
The Creator of all things?

Allah made us and the world around us.
We worship **Allah** and Him alone.

Worship means-
We pray to **Allah**
We bow to **Allah's** Glory
We bow to **Allah's** Power
We bow to **Allah's** Beauty
We praise **Allah**
We honour **Allah**
We obey **Allah**
We love **Allah**
We adore **Allah**
We fear **Allah**
All at once and in the best way.

We cannot pray or bow to anyone
but **Allah**.

All Muslims should do Salah,
or pray to **Allah**, 5 times a day.

We do Salah so **Allah** is happy with us,
and will show us the way of light.

When we do our Salah,
We face towards the Ka'bah or Qiblah.
The Ka'bah is the House of **Allah**
in Makkah.

The Ka'bah is a special place for Muslims.
It is a place of peace and calm thought.
From all over the world,
Muslims visit the city of Makkah
and walk around the Ka'bah.

The sun rises and the birds sing.
The gentle clouds that spread
across the sky
Hide the bright light of the sun.

When the clouds move away,
The happy sun smiles down on
the earth.

When the sun sets,
The smiling moon and the winking
stars shine bright.
They bring light to a sleeping night.

The mountains are high.
Beautiful are the fountains
and the blue sky.

The waterfalls gush forth.
The wind blows east, west, south and north.

The flowers grow, the rivers flow,
The trees stand tall, the rain drops fall.

Allah made them all.
They display His Beauty and Power.

Allah can see us.
We cannot see Him.
But we see the signs of Allah
All around us,
On the earth, in the skies and waters.

They help us to live.
They bring comfort and joy to us.

Allah made things in nature
To give us comfort and joy,
So they follow His command.

When Allah gives a command,
He gives us an order to do things.
We must then listen, follow and obey.

The command of Allah is called
Amr-e-Rabb in Arabic.

Allah is al-Basir,
He sees everything we do.

Allah is as-Sami,
He hears everything we say.

Allah is al-Alim,
He knows everything about everyone.

So it is very important
That Allah is happy with us.

How can we make Allah happy?

We can make **Allah** happy
By being good girls and boys.

By listening to our Mum and Dad,
By being a good sister
or a good brother.

By being nice to everyone,
Nice to our grandma and grandpa,
Nice to our aunt and uncle,
Nice to our cousins.

Nice to our friends,
Nice to our neighbours,
Nice to people in the streets,
Nice to people in the shops,
Nice to everyone everywhere.

If you are good girls and good boys,
You will listen to your teachers.
If you respect your teachers
Allah will be happy with you.

Mum and Dad are your teachers at home
and at school you have teachers.
They all teach you things you did not know.
They always want what is best for you.
They are all wise people.

When you make your parents
and teachers happy,
Then **Allah** is happy with you.

When **Allah** is happy with you,
He will give you the gift of barakah.

What is the gift of barakah?
It is a heaven-sent gift.
You cannot see it, but you can feel it.
It is a special feeling of
Peace and Happiness.

When **Allah** gives us barakah,
Nice things seem to happen to us
and everything seems pleasant
and delightful.

When **Allah** gives us barakah,
We should feel very lucky.

Allah also made angels.
What is an angel?
We are made of clay
but angels are made from light.
We cannot see them
but there are angels all around us.
They are called **malaikah** in Arabic.

Allah has made angels so that
They do not need to sleep or rest.
They are never hungry or thirsty,
So they do not eat or drink.
They keep busy with work all the time.
They carry out every command of **Allah**.
Angels always bow to the Glory of **Allah**.

We respect the angels by saying
alaihi-salam
After their name, which means
Peace be on him.

All the angels are truly noble and
pure beings.

There are angels who sing
Allah's glory and praise.

Angel Mikha'il *alaihi-salam* looks after
The holy places,
The favourite places of Allah.

There are visitor angels.
They visit places
and meetings of good people
who remember and praise Allah.

There are angels of good news.
They come down to earth to bless us,
Then return to Allah with news of us,
How we live,
What we do,
Whether we follow the way of Islam.

Angels are always ready
To help and protect us.
But we must always try our best
To be nice and to do good things.

The angels who stay with us all the time
and write down everything we do are called
Kiraman Katibeen (Noble writers).
They sit on our shoulders.

When we finish our Salah,
We turn our face to the right and
Then to the left and say
as-salam alaikum wa-rahmatullah.
This means *may* **Allah's**
peace and mercy be on you.

We are greeting the Kiraman Katibeen.

Special people called Prophets or
Messengers of Allah could see angels.

Who are the Prophets and Messengers
of Allah?

Allah chose certain people to tell us
How to obey and worship Him.

They were wise and great teachers and
They told us how to make Allah happy.

Almost 124,000 Prophets were sent
By Allah to teach people about Him.

Allah sent a Prophet to every nation
To teach them to worship and obey Him.

When people forgot to worship Allah,
He sent another Prophet to remind them.

We show respect to all the Prophets
By saying *alaihi-salam*
After each of their names.
This means *Peace be on him.*

We show special respect to our dear
Prophet Muhammad by saying
sallal-lahu-alaihi-wa-sallam.
This means:
Peace and blessings of Allah be on him.

The first Prophet was **Adam**
alaihi-salam
and the last Prophet was
Muhammad
sallal-lahu-alaihi-wa-sallam.

The Prophets whose names we know are:

Adam and Idris
Nuh and Hud and Salih
Ibrahim and his sons Isma'il and Ishaq
Lut
Yaqub and his son Yusuf
Shu'aib and Ayyub
Musa and his brother Harun
Dhul Kifl
Da'ud and his son Sulaiman
Ilyas and Al-Yasa
Yunus and Zakariyya
Isa and his cousin Yahya
(Peace be on them all)

**The final Prophet of Allah was
Prophet Muhammad**
sallal-lahu-alaihi-wa-sallam

All the Prophets worked very hard
To tell as many people as they could
About Allah and how to be good.
They were great teachers and wise people.

Prophet Muhammad
sallal-lahu-alaihi-wa-sallam
Was the best example to us all.

He was the final Messenger of Allah
We must respect him,
Honour him, praise him
and love him.

We can do this by following his example
and by doing what he told us to do.

26

Prophet Muhammad
sallal-lahu-alaihi-wa-sallam
Always spoke the truth,
So the people of his time called him
As-Sadiq, the truthful.

He was everyone's trusted friend,
So the people of his time called him
Al-Amin, the most trusted.

Our dear Prophet has other names:
Rasul-Allah or Messenger of **Allah**
Nabi-Allah or Prophet of **Allah**
Habib-Allah or Beloved of **Allah**

أحمد

Now I shall tell you more about
our dear Prophet.

When Muhammad Rasul-Allah was young,
Everyone called him Ahmad,
Ahmad means 'the one who praises',
Because he praised Allah.
He has taught us everything about Allah.
He has taught us about the light of Islam.

When he grew up,
Everyone called him Muhammad.
Muhammad means
'The one who is praised'.
He is praised by Allah and His angels
In the heavens and on earth.
Allah gave Rasul-Allah the highest honour.
We must praise him too.

محمد

Some Prophets or Nabi were given
a book by **Allah**. These special Prophets
are called Messengers or Rasul.

Now I shall tell you about
The Books of **Allah**.

Prophet Ibrahim *alaihi-salam*
was given the **SUHUF**.

Prophet Musa *alaihi-salam*
was given the **TAWRAT**.

Prophet Da'ud *alaihi-salam*
was given the **ZABUR**.

Prophet Isa *alaihi-salam*
was given the **INJEEL**.

Allah gave these books to His Rasul
as a gift for
their people.

SUHUF, TAWRAT, ZABUR and INJEEL
contained the Message of **Allah**.
But over time the Message of **Allah**
was lost.

So **Allah** gave to His final Messenger,
Prophet Muhammad
sallal-lahu-alaihi-wa-sallam
THE QUR'AN.

The QUR'AN is the final, the last
and the perfect message of **Allah**.

It is **Allah's** Noble Book.
It is **Allah's** gift to the Muslims through
Prophet Muhammad
sallal-lahu-alaihi-wa-sallam.

How did **Allah** give The QUR'AN
To Rasul-Allah
sallal-lahu-alaihi-wa-sallam?

The QUR'AN was brought to Rasul-Allah
By Angel Jibra'il *alaihi-salam*.
Jibra'il *alaihi-salam* visited
Rasul-Allah quite often.

Jibra'il *alaihi-salam* is a special angel.
The QUR'AN calls him
The 'holy' and 'trusted' angel.

Allah gave Jibra'il *alaihi-salam*
A very special task.
He was trusted to bring down
The QUR'AN to Rasul-Allah
sallal-lahu-alaihi-wa-sallam
To guide Muslims to Islam.

Rasul-Allah was in deep thought
In the Cave of Hira,
When Angel Jibra'il *alaihi-salam*
First came to him.

Angel Jibra'il *alaihi-salam* appeared
In a dazzling light.
All Hira lit up brilliant and bright.

Hira is in Jabl-e-Nur.
Jabl-e-Nur means the Mountain of Light.

From that day Rasul-Allah obeyed
The QUR'AN.
The QUR'AN is the word of **Allah**,
So Rasul-Allah obeyed **Allah**.
We must obey **Allah** too.

Allah is called Al-Majid and Al-Karim.
He is Glorious, He is Generous.

Allah tells us what to do and how to live
in His Heavenly Book.
It has two beautiful names:
Qur'an al-Majid - The Glorious QUR'AN
Qur'an al-Karim - The Generous QUR'AN

The QUR'AN is written in Arabic.

It is important that we should all
learn Arabic,
So that we can understand
what The QUR'AN says.

We should also try to read The QUR'AN
Everyday.

Do you know the first word of The QUR'AN
That Angel Jibra'il *alaihi-salam* said to
Rasul-Allah *sallal-lahu-alaihi-wa-sallam*?

The first word was Iqra.

Do you know what Iqra means?
It means to read, recite, learn,
study and think.

And what should we learn?
We should learn about **Allah**, the
Prophets, The QUR'AN and Islam.

Allah

Prophets

Qur'an

Islam

To be a good Muslim,
We must read, recite, learn, study, think;
Learn about Islam,
About the world around us,
About other people and how they live.

To be smart you must
Go to school, learn to read and write,
Do homework and work hard.
Then go out to play games
and have lots and lots of fun.

To be smart you must read story books,
Other good books and books on Islam.

Just as we came into this world,
We must all leave this world some day.

All of us have a soul.
It helps us to breathe.
It helps us to live.

When **Allah** gives the command,
Angel Izra'il *alaihi-salam* carries our
soul back to **Allah**.

When **Allah** takes our soul,
Our soul leaves our body to go back to Him.
Allah sends Angel Izra'il *alaihi-salam*
To take our breath away.

That is when we leave this world.

We must do everything we can
To make Allah happy now,
So that when we leave this world
Allah sends us to Heaven.

Heaven is more beautiful than any
place you can imagine.

Who decides if you go to Heaven?
Allah does.

When does He decide this?
On the Day of Judgement or the
Last Day.

What is the Last Day?

A day will come, far and far away,
When this entire world,
The earth and all the skies,
All the seas and all the oceans,
All the rivers and all the lakes,
All the mountains and all the fountains,
All the hills and all the valleys,
All the trees and all the flowers,
All the animals and all the beasts,
All the birds and all the ducks,
And each and every one of us,
And all the people that are yet to come,
And all the signs of **Allah** Most High,
Will stand before **Allah**.

Angel Israfeel *alaihi-salam*
Will blow the Trumpet twice,
To tell us that the time has come
For us to stand before **Allah**.

This will be on the Last Day.
It is the Day of Judgment,
It is the Day of Gathering,
When we will all gather together
At the end of our journey
Through this world.

On the Last Day,
If we have made **Allah** happy,
Then our faces will be shining with light
and **Allah** will send us to Heaven.

Angel Ridwan *alaihi-salam* is the angel
who looks after Heaven.

You can never be sad in Heaven.
You will never worry about anything
in Heaven.

You can stay in Heaven forever,
But only if you have been good.

So we have to be good to people.
Good to ourselves by being nice,
Good to others by being helpful.

We have to show respect
and gentle care for everything,
Because **Allah** has made
Everyone and every living thing.
Allah can see and hear everything.

A Muslim must be good to everyone.
If we want others to be nice to us,
Then we have to be good to them,
To show them respect,
To help them, to be kind to them.
This is an act of **charity**.

Do you know what **charity** means?
It means to give of yourself to others.
How do you give of yourself to others?
By being nice, by helping people,
By doing things for them,
Even if it is something very little.
This is the way of Islam.

If others hurt you my dear friends,
If they are not good to you,
You should pray to **Allah** for them,
So that they do not hurt you any more.

To pray for those
Who are not nice to us
is also a charity.
It means we are trying
To help others to be good.
Not to hurt back those who hurt us
is also a charity.

If they still hurt you,
Do not hurt them back.
Spend time with those
who are good to you.
This is the path of Islam.

Allah wants all Muslims to be very good.
If we are good
Allah will be happy with us,
Allah will show us respect,
Allah will give us barakah:
The most precious gift in life.

BARAKAH
from
Allah

Remember, if we want our faces to
shine with light,
We must do as Allah asks us to do.

An-Noor means Light.
An-Noor is a name of **Allah**.

Allah is the Light of the Heavens and
Earth

The **QUR'AN** is Light.
The word of **Allah** is the Light.
Islam is the Light.

The QUR'AN calls Rasul-Allah
a light giving lamp.

What happens when we switch on
a lamp in a dark room?
The lamp spreads light across the room,
Like the stars and the moon that
Shine at night helping travellers
Find their way in the darkness.

Before Islam the world was in darkness.
No prophet had come for a long time
To teach people the good way.

In this dark time Rasul-Allah came
To teach people the light of Islam,
So that Muslims could find their way
To travel to the path of Islam.

The Prophet Muhammad
sallal-lahu-alaihi-wa-sallam
said a very special prayer:

اللَّهُمَّ اجْعَلْ فِي قَلْبِي نُورًا، وَفِي بَصَرِي نُورًا،

وَفِي سَمْعِي نُورًا، وَعَنْ يَمِينِي نُورًا، وَعَنْ يَسَارِي نُورًا،

وَفَوْقِي نُورًا، وَتَحْتِي نُورًا، وَأَمَامِي نُورًا،

وَخَلْفِي نُورًا، وَاجْعَلْ لِي نُورًا،

"O **Allah,**
Place a light in my heart,
A light in my hearing,
A light in my seeing,
A light on my right hand,
A light on my left hand,
A light before me, A light behind me,
A light above me, A light below me,
And choose for me a light."

This is called the Prayer of Light.
Our dear Prophet was very fond
of this prayer.
This is a very beautiful prayer.

It is a prayer of peace that we ask of
Allah.
We ask Him to bless us.

I hope you will read this prayer too.
If you say this prayer,
If **Allah** wants, you will have
Lots and lots of barakah,
And **Allah** will choose for you
A beautiful light.